The Reckoning
That Counts

The Reckoning
That Counts

The Realization of Spiritual Growth

Miles J. Stanford

OF THE ZONDERVAN CORPORATION
GRAND RAPIDS, MICHIGAN 49506

THE RECKONING THAT COUNTS
© 1977 by Miles Stanford
First published in 1966

Library of Congress Cataloging in Publication Data

Stanford, Miles J
    The reckoning that counts.

    (His The "green letters" series)
    1. Christian life — 1960-   I. Title.   II. Series.
BV4501.2.S719   248'.4   76-39688

Printed in the United States of America

CONTENTS

Preface

PREFACE

The Reckoning That Counts, fourth in *The Green Letters* series, is shared with the assurance that there are many of the Lord's hungry-hearted ones who are aware of their need to understand more fully what the call to "reckon" involves, as found in Romans 6:11.

We are trusting the Lord to prepare each heart and mind that takes up this brief study. Reckoning is predicated upon that which one already knows — it is to count upon the truth which is known and understood.

There must be Spirit-dependent study and concentration on the part of the believer if he is to enter into the spiritual growth that is realized through reckoning.

"And now, brethren, I commend you to God, and to the word of his grace, which is able to build you up, and to give you an inheritance among all them which are sanctified" (Acts 20:32).

—MILES J. STANFORD

Colorado Springs
Colorado

The Reckoning
That Counts

Chapter 1

Principles of Reckoning

The purpose of *The Green Letters* was to set forth the truths of identification, as well as some of the basic principles by which God brings us into their reality.

As a sequel to the *Letters*, this study deals with the essential principles having to do with our *reckoning* upon the identification truths. It is an attempt to answer the question, "*How* do I reckon?"

To facilitate our understanding of the subject, we will define at the outset the three basic elements of the reckoning that counts.

Principles

According to Webster, a principle is "the law of nature [or the method] by which a thing operates." The *how* of reckoning is based on principles. Our Father works according to His spiritual principles to fulfill His purpose in our lives. For example: He brings us into the reality of our identification on the basis of *the principle of knowledge* (know the scriptural truths), *the principle of faith* (reckon upon the truths known), and *the principle of time* (yield to His lifetime processing for growth in the truths known and reckoned upon).

Identification With Christ

The truths of identification are those facts in the Word which reveal our identification with Christ in His death unto sin, and our subsequent re-creation in His resurrection. As foreknown believers, our Father judicially placed us in His Son on the cross — so that we died in Him unto sin, and are now alive in Him unto God.

Reckon

The word means "to regard as being, to count as true." Romans 6:11 calls upon us to count upon the truths of our identification with Christ: "Reckon ye also yourselves to be dead unto sin, but alive unto God in Christ Jesus" (ASV). We count upon the truth that is made known to us; we exercise faith by resting upon the facts.

It may be helpful to observe that there is a *pattern* throughout our spiritual development. Whether it was realized or not, we began to "reckon" at the very beginning of our Christian life. As lost sinners, we were convicted of our need and shown in the Word that the Savior died on the cross to redeem us. By His grace we reckoned upon the truth, and received Him as our personal Savior.

With hearts full of love and zeal, we became active for the Lord as the new life began to emerge. All went well for a time, possibly several years. Then, imperceptibly, a deadly declension set in. We had been so busy enjoying the new experience and activities that we inadvertently began to neglect the Source of all true life and service — both the written and the Living Word. The inevitable result was the reassertion of the enslaving influence of sin, self, law, and the world. Almost before we realized it, we were defeated, heartsick, and wretched.

Finally, after years of failure in both life and service, we were prepared to see something of the wonderful truths concerning our identification with the Lord Jesus Christ in His death and resurrection. We saw that He not only freed us from the guilt and penalty of sin, but also from the power and domination of *the principle of sin*. Here we see the pattern of the experience of "babes in Christ": we believed, we struggled, we failed.

Now, what of the pattern of our adulthood, when we come to the place of reckoning upon the identification truths? Just as in our counting upon the justification truths for the initial steps of birth and babyhood, so in our reckoning upon the identification truths for growth: we start immediately to work for the Lord in testifying of our new experience. We want everyone to know of our new joy and freedom through reckoning.

Not only do we seek out opportunities to share and teach these new-to-us truths, but, where necessary, we *make* openings. We are surprised to discover that few, if any, fellow-believers prove to be receptive. As a matter of fact, many become antagonistic, and some even accuse us of falling into error. There are times when we limp home not quite as sure or enthusiastic about it all as when we started.

Then too, we begin to grow careless about our reckoning. We forget about the liberating truths for longer and longer periods of time. Once again we are relying more upon our experience than we are upon our Source (the risen Christ) and the means (reckoning) of receiving His abundant life. And what is the sure result of concentrating upon experience rather than truth? Defeat! Thus the pattern is completed: our failure in the identification realm parallels our failure in the earlier justification phase.

At just this point many believers begin to waver in their

hope and expectation of freedom from the old life and abundant growth in the new. Their confidence in the truths of identification begins to wane. How many defeated Christians have exclaimed bitterly, "I *tried* Romans Six, but reckoning didn't work for me"!

Most discouraged ones turn back to the futile struggles of Romans Seven as a result of this seeming failure. Some even follow the alluring experience-centered errors of the so-called "holiness" groups. But whatever it may be, all, all outside the realm of Spirit-taught and Spirit-ministered identification truth results in compounded failure and bondage. "Having begun in the Spirit, are ye now made perfect [mature] in the flesh?" (Gal. 3:3).

Patterns spring from principles. There is a definite and essential principle underlying this pattern of seeing the truth, reckoning upon it, experiencing the good of it for a time, and then — failure. Therefore, take heart, fellow-believer, for our Father is ever working according to His principles, patterns, and purpose for us.

When the Holy Spirit brings us to a new and higher plateau of truth in the process of our growth, we see, we reckon upon, we appropriate that which we understand. But the important thing to remember is that this is only the beginning of a new spiritual plane. At the outset of our reckoning upon the identification truths, all is exciting and wonderful, and we are given a taste of the reality of these facts we are counting upon. However, tasting is not eating. This initial experience is but a *token* of all that lies ahead in the long, slow, growing process. Our early enthusiasm makes it all seem clear and simple, but there are infinite depths and heights in every realm of truth into which He intends to bring us and establish us. This will require both time, and eternity.

Hence, the Holy Spirit allows us to fail after our eager beginning. He applies *the principle of need* in every phase of our advance. The calculated failure is used to cause us to move beyond the early infant-enthusiasm to the place where we have to dig in and settle down upon the explicit truth of the Word. Before we can grow in any aspect of truth, we must be established in the knowledge of it. In every area of our spiritual development, it is one thing to begin on a new plateau, but it is quite another thing "through faith and patience to inherit the promises" (Heb. 6:12).

Our immaturity was understandable during the "milk-of-the-gospel" stage of our Christian life, but now it is time to face up to adulthood. We have partaken of the meat of identification. "Strong meat belongeth to them that are of full age, even those who by reason of use have their senses exercised to discern both good and evil" (Heb. 5:14). In our need and desperation we grasp a truth, but our initial knowledge is insufficient to enable us to persevere in it. To cause the truth to take hold of us and become a living part of our life, the Holy Spirit removes the token experience from us — but the knowledge of the truth is retained. By this means we are to be *established in the truth*, that we might "grow in grace, and in the knowledge of our Lord and Saviour Jesus Christ" (2 Pet. 3:18). The first taste of identification awakens our heart-hunger for its practical fulfillment. "I follow after, if that I may apprehend that for which also I am apprehended of Christ Jesus" (Phil. 3:12).

It will help us to bear in mind that *the principle of time* underlies all of God's dealings with us. Growth takes time!

15

"The God of all grace, who hath called us unto His eternal glory by Christ Jesus, after that ye have suffered a while, make you perfect [mature], stablish, strengthen, settle you" (1 Pet. 5:10).

Chapter 2

Three Steps in Reckoning

Everything that has to do with our Christian life, including the longed-for freedom from the power of sin and self is *in* our Lord Jesus Christ. Through our spiritual birth in Him, we know Him in His person to be the very *source* of our life. "Your life is hid with Christ in God . . . . Christ, who is our life" (Col. 3:3,4).

Now, failure in reckoning is certainly not failure of the truths reckoned upon. Never! Without the Scriptures we would have absolutely nothing. Our authoritative Bible is the only means in the universe by which we can ever know anything rightly and personally of the Father, the Son, and the Holy Spirit. Sad to say, even with the revealed Word, there is little enough of this all-important spiritual knowledge among believers today.

We should remind ourselves that the written Word was designed specifically by God to bring us to know the Living Word. Never for a moment is the written revelation to be by-passed, or slighted in any way. We are to study, meditate, and count upon it through the ministry of the Spirit of Truth, in order that we may know the Lord Jesus. He is our all, *by means of the Word.* "His divine power hath given unto us all things that pertain unto life and godliness, through the knowledge of him that hath called us to glory and virtue: whereby are given unto us exceeding great and precious

17

promises: *that by these* ye might be partakers of the divine nature." "By him all things consist. And he is the head of the body." "For in him dwelleth all the fulness of the Godhead bodily" (2 Pet. 1:3,4; Col. 1:17,18; 2:9).

Surely, it can be affirmed that the written Truth, authored and administered by the Holy Spirit, is the "vehicle" by which the Father and the Son come to us, and we to them. Still, as to reckoning upon the specific identification truths centered in Romans Six, nearly all of us *stop* at the written Word. It is as though we stand there, with a deathgrip on a handful of truth, repeating with conviction: "I believe this is true, and I reckon, reckon, reckon!"

Much of the failure of our reckoning is due to *erroneous expectation*. We are not delivered by belief only in the liberation truths! Certainly we must believe and appropriate these truths, but the actual liberation comes as the result of our intimate, personal fellowship with the Lord Jesus through the Holy Spirit. Simply put, the principle is: *liberation is in the Liberator*.

The reckoning that counts is made up of three essential steps. Most believers stop at the first, many stop at the second, but none can know the true results of reckoning apart from reliance upon all three factors. Our freedom from domination by the sinful Adamic life was completed *positionally* through our identification with the Lord Jesus on Calvary. There we shared His death unto sin, and from there we entered into His life unto God. From this eternal position in Christ, our *experiential* freedom and growth are carried out as we: (1) Know, and reckon upon, the identification truths; (2) Abide, and rest, in our Liberator; (3) Depend upon, and walk in, the Spirit. Not just the first step, not even

18

the first and second, but all three comprise the walk of reckoning!

(1) *Know and Reckon*

When we first realize our identification with the Lord Jesus according to Romans 6:1-10, we begin to count upon these wonderful truths as we are enjoined in verse 11. Often there is a definite crisis in the life at this time, as some emancipation from bondage is experienced. But it isn't long before most "reckoners" go into spiritual shock; they do not understand that this initial taste of liberation is but a strengthening vision, a brief time of knowing something of what lies ahead. Our Lord removes fluctuating experience so that eternal truth, clear and steady, may be our foundation. We are not to rely upon *experiences* for growth and maturity, no matter how wonderful and stimulating they seem to be.

As we learn more of the truth upon which we are reckoning, our knowledge becomes a set heart-attitude: I have died unto sin; I am alive in Christ unto God (Rom. 6:11). Although our initial reckoning may bring blessing, its primary purpose is to foster *the twofold process of growth:* "always delivered unto *death* . . . that the *life* also of Jesus might be made manifest in our mortal flesh [body]" (2 Cor. 4:11, italics ours).

(2) *Abide and Rest*

Each of us must become aware of our union of life in the risen Lord; we are a branch in the True Vine. By means of this awareness we learn to abide. We simply rest where we have been newly created — in Christ. "Abide in me, and I in you. As the branch cannot bear fruit of itself, except it abide

19

in the vine; no more can ye, except ye abide in me. I am the vine, ye are the branches: he that abideth in me, and I in him, the same bringeth forth much fruit: for without me ye can do nothing" (John 15:4,5). Not only is the written Word to be counted upon, but the Living Word is to be rested in.

(3) *Depend and Walk*

The liberating principle is fully embraced by including the final step: walking in dependence upon the Holy Spirit. Deep within our spirit He abides forever, and there, through our study, He teaches us the truth of our position. Then, as we reckon upon the truth taught, He applies the crucifixion of the cross to the old man, and ministers the life of Christ to the new. "Walk in [depend upon] the Spirit, and ye shall not fulfil the lust of the flesh." "For the law of the Spirit of life in Christ Jesus hath made me free from the law of sin and death" (Gal. 5:16; Rom. 8:2). Our reckoning becomes effective as we count upon the Word, abide in the Lord, and walk in the Spirit.

Another subtle reason why our reckoning flounders in the midst of these steps is that our *motives* are centered in self. We know and count upon identification for *our* liberation; we abide and rest in Him for *our* growth and peace; and we seek to depend upon and walk in the Spirit for *our* empowering and fruitfulness. Is it any wonder we have to be child-trained and led into a Christ-centered attitude? The Father's purpose in justifying us in Christ and identifying us with Him is that we might be "conformed to the image of his Son" — "that *God* in all things may be glorified through Jesus Christ" (Rom. 8:29; 1 Pet. 4:11).

The following example from the experience of Jacob

illustrates God's method of *centering our hearts in Himself*. In this instance, He accomplished the spiritual by means of the physical.

The wily, self-centered Jacob had taken the correct steps, and he was "in the land." But he still had to be turned from Jacob, to God. He needed to be rendered helpless in himself, to become wholly dependent upon God. The long night of the Father's dealings ("He touched the hollow of his thigh; and the hollow of Jacob's thigh was out of joint") was coupled with Jacob's trusting and tenacious wrestlings with God ("I will not let Thee go, except Thou bless me"). Through the merciful chastening of God, Jacob finally came to see his need. "And He blessed him there . . . and he halted upon his thigh." God blessed Jacob by crippling him in himself, thereby enabling him to limp the remainder of his life in blessed dependence upon God; he was God-centered. He was brought all the way from Jacob, the supplanter, to Israel, a prince with God. "Thy name shall be called no more Jacob, but Israel: for as a prince hast thou power with God and with men, and hast prevailed" (Gen. 32:24-29).

It is through this same *principle of strength out of weakness* that we are developed in the "not I, but Christ" life. "For my strength is made perfect in [your] weakness" (2 Cor. 12:7,9).

Chapter 3

Knowledge of Reckoning

Knowledge of scriptural truth should precede spiritual growth. For example, in the early chapters of Paul's epistles doctrinal truth is presented, while the latter chapters deal with the practical results of the truth set forth. We must first know what the triune God has done, before we can count upon Him to "do." "That the God of our Lord Jesus Christ, the Father of glory, may give unto you the spirit of wisdom and revelation in the *knowledge* of him"; "For it is God which *worketh* in you both to will and to do of his good pleasure" (Eph. 1:17; Phil. 2:13).

There is a crippling tendency among believers today to deprecate head-knowledge of the truth, and even doctrine itself. Emphasis is being put on so-called heart-knowledge gained by means of experience. This, however, is to place condition before position, which is the opposite of God's scriptural pattern. Truth reckoned upon fosters the only healthy and abiding spiritual experience. For faith to function, there must be Spirit-given knowledge of the Word.

The Spirit of Truth ministers truth to us by means of our mind — the spiritual mind that relies upon Him. This head-knowledge gives us the facts upon which we exercise faith, or reckon. In time, through deeper understanding and a quiet assimilation of the truth, there is both head-knowledge and heart-knowledge: we not only believe, but now we know experientially. Paul had believed on the Lord Jesus for many years before he wrote, "That I may *know* him" (Phil. 3:10). Likewise, he urges us to "Meditate upon these things; give thyself wholly to them; that thy profiting may appear to all" (1 Tim. 4:15). For, as a man "thinketh within himself, so is he" (Prov. 23:7, ASV).

Some people belittle head-knowledge because they see many Christians who seem to know so much Scripture yet whose lives fail to "adorn the doctrine" (Titus 2:10). Doubtless there is some justification for this reaction, but it should be realized that one's knowledge of truth is always in advance of his growth in that truth. Many believers know truth in which it will take them a lifetime (and eternity) to grow.

Further, there are those on every hand who know *about* truth, having grasped and even memorized Scripture by means of the natural mind. Such knowledge will never become living experience. In the final analysis, we are not to decide about spiritual matters by observation of other believers. It is the Holy Spirit who must teach us by means of the Word, "comparing spiritual things with spiritual" (1 Cor. 2:13).

Paul states that there are some who have "a zeal for God, but not according to knowledge" (Rom. 10:2, ASV). Ideally, head-knowledge precedes heart-knowledge. However, neither one is preeminent above the other — both are essential for *healthy growth* and *effective ministry*. Heart-knowledge alone cannot progress beyond the fluctuating feelings and emotions of babyhood. It can exhort, emotionalize, and share experiences and blessings, but it cannot lead others to establishment in the truth. To share effectively, we must be brought to maturity of both head- and heart-knowledge.

We are to reckon and stand upon certain truths for our *foundation.* Linked with these are other truths upon which we are to reckon and rest for *growth.*

Foundation

There can be no growth unto maturity without an established foundation. By knowledge of the Word we are anchored and rooted in the eternal foundation of our Christian life: (1) *Born anew in Christ:* "Born again, not of corruptible seed, but of incorruptible, by the Word of God, which liveth and abideth forever" (1 Pet. 1:23). (2) *Accepted in Christ* (our Father is able to accept us fully in His Son): "To the praise of the glory of his grace, wherein he hath made us accepted in the beloved" (Eph. 1:6). (3) *Eternally secured in Christ:* "Your life is hid with Christ in God" (Col. 3:3). (4) *Positioned in Christ:* "God . . . hath quickened [enlifed] us together with Christ . . . and hath raised us up together and made us sit together in heavenly places in Christ Jesus" (Eph. 2:4-6). It is futile to seek to grow by means of these truths — they are foundational. But it is imperative that we grow *upon* this imperishable foundation.

Growth

Once we receive the head- and heart-knowledge by which we are established upon our foundation in Christ, the question of growth in Him is all but settled. The deeper truth, the spiritual master-key to all growth and maturity, is the fact that we are not only founded in Him, but that we are *complete in Him.* "For in Him dwelleth all the fulness of the Godhead bodily. And ye are complete in Him" (Col. 2:9,10). As the Holy Spirit gives us the knowledge of our position in Christ, we are prepared to know Him as our *Life* (Col. 3:4). To reckon himself "alive unto God in Christ," the branch must know the True Vine as his complete source of life. "Of him are ye in Christ Jesus, who of God is made unto us wisdom, and righteousness, and sanctification, and redemption" (1 Cor. 1:30). To reckon upon the truth is to rest in, and receive the fruit of, the truth.

Can we now see where the failure began in our Christian walk? We had the knowledge of the justification truths for our new birth, and upon this "milk of the gospel" we sought to grow and serve. But there was defeat, because the foundation truths are for beginning only. Further knowledge was our need. We had simply *gone beyond our teaching!* We knew the Lord Jesus as our Foundation, but not as our Life.

The same problem exists in many of our early attempts to reckon upon the identification truths. We seek to reckon ourselves dead unto sin without being established in the knowledge of the cross. The failure is further compounded by our seeking to reckon ourselves alive unto God in Christ without first being established in the knowledge of Him as our risen Life. We must be established in the knowledge of our foundation and source, if we are to become established in our reckoning and growth.

There are three pillars of knowledge having to do with *position* upon which the Christian life is to be secured and matured.

The First Pillar

The knowledge of our birth, acceptance, and security in the Lord Jesus Christ is the first pillar.

The Second Pillar

The knowledge of His cross as our cross is the central pillar. The cross of Calvary is not only the central fact of the universe, but also of the life of the believer. As we see our identification with Christ in His death unto sin, we know His cross to be our cross. We know self to have been crucified there; we know ourselves to have been cut off from Adam and freed from the power of sin. Only from this pillar of knowledge can we reckon ourselves dead unto sin in our daily walk.

The Third Pillar

The knowledge that we are alive, and complete, in our risen Lord places us securely upon the third pillar. Now our reckoning can be fully established, as we count ourselves to be alive unto God in Christ. Now His life can be manifested in us by the growing fruit of the Spirit. This is the practical fulfillment of the very purpose of God for us: that we be conformed to the image of His Son.

Chapter 4

Spirit-applied
Reckoning

"The Comforter, even the Holy Spirit . . . he shall teach you all things . . . . He shall glorify me: for he shall take of mine, and shall declare it unto you" (John 14:26; 16:14, ASV).

"The Comforter, even the Holy Spirit." The Lord Jesus chose the perfect designation in introducing the Holy Spirit as our Comforter. Even in our sin, He comforts us. True, He convicts us of sin — and Holy Spirit conviction can be intense — but He does so in order to point us to the Blood which ever cleanses us from all sin, and to the Lord Jesus who is the propitiation for our sins, the One who ever lives to make intercession for us (1 John 1:7; 2:1,2; Heb. 7:25). The enemy condemns us when we sin, and seeks to crush us under the weight of guilt. But the Comforter does not condemn; He convicts so that we might confess and be cleansed from all unrighteousness (1 John 1:9).

When it comes to reckoning, we need the Holy Spirit as our Comforter more than ever. We are quite surprised when we begin to realize how much suffering is involved in reckoning. We cannot reckon ourselves "to be dead indeed unto sin" without experiencing the deep, inner crucifixion of the cross as it is applied to the self-life. The dual truth upon which the Spirit has us reckon is that which He makes experiential in our lives: (1) We count upon having died unto

27

sin, and are "alway delivered unto death" as the outworking of that position of death; (2) we count upon being alive unto God in Christ, and the Spirit causes "the life also of Jesus to be manifested in our mortal flesh" (2 Cor. 4:11).

All spiritual growth entails a lifelong *process*. We have an infinite Lord as our life, to whose image we are being conformed by the Eternal Spirit. Our dire need causes us to long for and expect immediate emancipation and newness of life as a result of our reckoning. To a degree, the Spirit complies with this expectation during our early encounter with identification. But He must bring us into the process of growth.

Consider the pattern of the Mount of Transfiguration experience. Although Peter, James, and John were given the glorious privilege of beholding the Lord Jesus transfigured, each one had to come down from the Mount — the Lord Jesus and Peter going to crosses, James to the sword, and John exiled to lonely Patmos. The same principle applies to us. We are given a glimpse of the glory and reality of the truth reckoned upon, and then we are taken into God's processing so that the truth may be as real *in* us as it is *to* us.

Through His purposeful dealings with us, our objective reckoning upon the truth becomes subjective experience in our lives. As we count upon our old man having been crucified at Calvary, and our having died unto sin on the cross, we become progressively cross-centered Christians. As we count upon our new life in the Lord Jesus, we develop into Christ-centered Christians. The path of the cross is the path of growth.

In our failures, we learn more of what *self* is and thereby come to hate the natural, Adamic life. Then it is that we are taught to glory in the cross, by which we are freed from the old life's influence, as well as the grip and lure of this *world*. "God forbid that I should glory, save in the cross of our Lord Jesus Christ, by whom the world is crucified unto me, and I unto the world" (Gal. 6:14). Reckoning is the only means of escaping the entanglements of this world. It takes the separation of the cross, and our abiding in Christ.

As the Holy Spirit applies the cross within, He takes us through difficulties and chastenings. We must face up to the fact that the cross has only suffering and death as its ministry. But when we realize that "alway delivered unto death" means the daily crucifixion of self, we begin to glory in the resultant freedom. "Now no chastening [child-training] for the present seemeth to be joyous, but grievous: nevertheless afterward it yieldeth the peaceable fruit of righteousness unto them which are exercised thereby" (Heb. 12:11). If we are going to receive the benefit of the cross, we must go through the suffering of the cross. That is where we come to know and appreciate the Holy Spirit as our Comforter. He comforts us in the very crucifixion He applies, and we learn to glory in the cross that crucifies. The work of the cross causes us to "rejoice in Christ Jesus, and have no confidence in the flesh" (Phil. 3:3).

"He shall teach you all things." It is often the case that hungry believers, needy as they know themselves to be, are more eager for experience than they are for revelation. They want a minimum of truth and study, with a maximum of results. But the more experience-centered they become, the less truth-established they will be. The penalty of this wrong emphasis is self-centeredness instead of Christ-centeredness.

This sad and selfish condition develops when *we* endeavor to handle and control the truth that we see. But the

29

truth of the Word does not respond to self. "The natural man receiveth not the things of the Spirit of God . . . neither can he know them, because they are spiritually discerned" (1 Cor. 2:14). As we study, we are to rest in the Spirit of life in Christ. The Lord Jesus said, "The Spirit of truth . . . will guide you into all truth" (John 16:13). There are those who even go so far as to attempt to use the Spirit. They want Him to give them "power," and many other self-centered "experiences" and "blessings." The Holy Spirit does not respond to such unholy aspirations.

"*He shall glorify Me: for He shall take of Mine, and shall declare it unto you.*" In all the vital work of the Holy Spirit in the Body of Christ, His intention and purpose is to glorify the Son in the individual members. The Lord Jesus prayed to His Father, "I pray not for the world, but for them which thou hast given me; for they are thine. And all mine are thine, and thine are mine; and I am glorified in them" (John 17:9,10).

How is He glorified in redeemed sinners? Our new birth means that each one of us is a new creation in Christ, at which time the Comforter enters our spirit to abide forever (John 14:16). Spirit to spirit joined, we are "partakers of the divine nature." At birth we are "babes in Christ," but as we grow in Him we develop in likeness of life — thus glorifying the Son.

The Holy Spirit receives the life of Christ and brings Him into our regenerated spirit. For that life to develop within, He reveals to us the Lord Jesus in the Word. Thus, feeding on Him in the Scriptures under the illumination of the Spirit of Truth, the new life in Christ grows and is made manifest in our mortal body. We grow in Him as we allow the Holy Spirit to show Him to us. "We all, with open face beholding as in a glass the glory of the Lord, are changed into the same image from glory to glory, even as by the Spirit of the Lord" (2 Cor. 3:18).

In the midst of finding out about ourselves, we are to be especially aware of what we are in our Lord Jesus. While the Spirit must cause us suffering in the crucifixion of the self-life, He comforts us in our growth in the new life. "Take, my brethren, the prophets, who have spoken in the name of the Lord, for an example of suffering affliction, and of patience. Behold, we count them happy which endure. Ye have heard of the patience of Job, and have seen the end of the Lord; that the Lord is very pitiful, and of tender mercy" (James 5:10,11).

As we turn from the old man by reckoning upon the work of the cross, we turn to the new man in Christ by reckoning upon the work of the Spirit. Gradually, as we grow, there are less and less "works of the flesh" evident, and more and more of the "fruit of the Spirit" manifested in our daily walk (Gal. 5:19,22).

What comfort there is in the faithful work of the Comforter! In the natural realm, a worm is changed into a butterfly — a different creature, but of the same order of life. In the spiritual realm, a believer is reborn — a totally *"new creation* in Christ Jesus" (2 Cor. 5:17, margin). Therefore, we "yield ourselves unto God, as those that are alive from the dead," and in dependence upon the Comforter we "walk in *newness* of life" (Rom. 6:13, 4).

Chapter 5

Service and Reckoning

Most of us have been warned at one time or another about "the barrenness of a busy life." Well-intentioned as the admonition may be, busyness does not necessarily produce a barren life. Rather, *barrenness of life produces busyness!*

The majority of active members in our sound churches today are primarily doers; their chief concern is to work for the Lord. But, service being the emphasis of their life, they are for the most part motivated by self. We must all learn, sooner or later, that the result of every form of self-effort is nothing but a barren waste, a spiritual Death Valley. Our growth is bound to falter and dry up when service is predominant in the life, especially in the formative years. Conversely, when *growth in Christ* is given first place, service will never suffer. Furthermore, our life-work will be accomplished in His time and way — and that without physical, mental, or spiritual breakdown.

The tragedy of the church is that the service-centered believer has little or no concern for spiritual growth, other than enough development and training for what he and others consider to be fruitful service. Naturally altruistic, he is appalled at the thought of placing growth ahead of outreach. The activist rarely seems to become aware of the sin of self, of the necessity of the cross in his life, or of God's purpose for him to be conformed to the image of Christ.

There are many believers who feel that the chief problem in our congregations is the existence of an overwhelming number of pew parasites. But, on the other hand, the vast army of busy-bee workers in our midst constitutes a comparable problem. Both doing nothing, and doing over-much, are a hindrance to God's purpose. His will for the Christian is expressed in the word *being*, which in turn will result in effective *doing*.

The reason for this reversal of God's order is plain to see. The emphasis of the average sound ministry is on salvation and service. Get saved, and get busy! This makes the new birth everything, and service its by-product. With this approach, the individual has practically reached his goal at the very outset. He is saved, and joins the church, then settles down to await his eternal reward. He attends sporadically, but must constantly be "attended to." On the other hand are those who do all the work, consequently having little time or hunger to "grow in grace and in the knowledge of our Lord and Saviour Jesus Christ" (2 Pet. 3:18).

Our Father's *ultimate purpose* in saving us is that we might be conformed to the image of His Son, not simply to keep us out of hell and get us into heaven. We have been born into Christ that He may be our *life*, not just our Savior. "For we know that all things work together for good to them that love God, to them who are the called according to his purpose. For whom he did foreknow, he also did predestinate to be conformed to the image of his Son" (Rom. 8:28,29).

When we realize that we have been born into the Lord Jesus so that His life "might be made manifest in our mortal flesh," our heart-hunger is brought into harmony with that of the Spirit for us: "changed into the same image from glory to

33

glory, even as by the Spirit of the Lord" (2 Cor. 3:18). "Can two walk together, except they be agreed?" (Amos 3:3). Our burden for ourselves and others will be the same as the Holy Spirit placed upon Paul's heart: "My little children, of whom I travail in birth again until Christ be formed in you" (Gal. 4:19). The emphasis of our life will be growth in Christ; the result of that growth will be fruitful and abiding service for His glory.

In our early years most of us place service far ahead of growth. It is true that there are "results" of a sort during this period, but the main lesson we learn in all this eager activity is how *not* to do things. We are quietly being taught and trained by the Spirit through failure. After a time, our soul-winning becomes more difficult; there are not as many "decisions" as there once were. Worse still, most of these decisions turn out to be just that, and nothing more. Our natural reaction is to place the blame upon those with whom we deal, but the patient Holy Spirit finally enables us to face up to the fact that *we* are the hindrance. We are failures after all; we cannot serve acceptably.

It is usually this Spirit-planned failure in service by which we are brought to realize our need for growth and maturity. Then arises the heart-burden to become conformed to His image, and have Him do His work through us. The extended Romans Seven failure in this realm also is the Spirit's means of bringing us to the responsibility of reckoning. Instead of struggle and work, resulting in failure, the pattern becomes reckon and rest, resulting in growth.

Certainly we seek to keep the lost from going to hell, by winning them to the Savior. However, our responsibility in service is not to force decisions, but to allow the Holy Spirit to beget healthy souls through the Word and the testimony of our lives. We are first to be *witnesses*, then soul-winners. When the Lord Jesus is reigning and manifest in us, others will hunger for Him: "Sir, we would see Jesus" (John 12:21). When the Holy Spirit has convicted them of their need for the Savior, they will freely exercise "repentance toward God, and faith in our Lord Jesus Christ" (Acts 20:21). Thus, they will not be badgered into a decision to get saved before they are convicted of being lost; neither will they be coming to Him to get, but to give. At his conversion, Paul, "trembling and astonished said, *Lord*, what wilt thou have me to do?" (Acts 9:6).

This pattern of service is outlined in the Word. In Acts 2:32, Peter said, "This Jesus hath God raised up, whereof we all are *witnesses*." The Holy Spirit used witnesses to convict hearts concerning Christ. "Now when they heard this, they were pricked in their heart, and said unto Peter and to the rest of the apostles, Men and brethren, what shall we do?" (vs. 37). When hearts were convicted of sin through the loving boldness of believers and the witness of the Word, and they reached out, "*Then* Peter said unto them, . . . Repent . . . " (vs. 38). There was no actual soul-winning attempt until Peter's witness had effectively prepared hearts, then "the Lord added to the church daily such as should be saved" (vs. 47).

When our witnessing and personal work is under the control of the Holy Spirit, the burden and aim of our outreach will be not only that others may be brought to the Lord Jesus, but that they may be built up in Him. "Rooted and built up in him, and stablished in the faith, as ye have been taught, abounding therein with thanksgiving" (Col. 2:7). For

35

one thing, this will eliminate much of the heartache and devastation caused by so many falling by the wayside. When we have in mind the Father's ultimate purpose for each one, from the outset of our witnessing, there will be prayerful and careful Spirit-motivated preparation of hearts both *before* and *after* conversion.

The Lord Jesus is to be manifested in us for effective witnessing; He must be free to minister through us for fruitful soul-winning. Responsible service can be on no lesser basis. Others have every right to witness something *of* Him before deciding *about* Him. "Thanks be unto God, who always leadeth us in triumph in Christ, and maketh manifest through us the savor of his knowledge in every place" (2 Cor. 2:14, ASV).

Chapter 6

Romans Six
Reckoning

When we first encounter the identification truths, the most serious mistake we can make is to try to reckon *ourselves* to be dead. Surprising as it may be to some, the Word does not teach that we are to reckon thus! Neither does it teach that the world, the flesh, and the devil are to be reckoned dead.

It is quite common for the awakened believer, one who is yearning for the liberation of the cross in his life, to concentrate upon reckoning himself to be dead. He is sincere about fully entering into this first aspect of identification. Although he is still aware of the old life within, he feels that if he just reckons upon his death in Christ intently and consistently he will in time come to the place where there is no longer any response to sin and self.

Others press this matter a step further, claiming that self is dead at the very outset of their reckoning it so. To uphold this claim, any subsequent manifestation of sin or self in the life is to them "just a shadow cast by the enemy"; they do not consider it to be sin. Also, these uprisings of sin within are considered to be simply "old habits seeking to reassert themselves," which they feel will soon be replaced by the development of new, righteous habits.

But this desired result cannot follow, as the entire principle is erroneous. Sad to say, the problem of faulty reckoning in this instance, due to a wrong interpretation, is mainly caused by an inferior translation in our beloved King James Version. In Romans 6:6 the word "destroyed" is used in reference to "the body of sin" (the law of sin in our members), thereby causing many to take for granted that self is dead and gone once they begin to reckon it so.

In the first place, the content of Romans Six has to do with the tyrannical reign of *the principle of sin* — not its symptom, sins. The problem of sins has been dealt with at the source by the crucifixion of the cross. The King James Version's use of "destroyed" in verse 6 is far too strong for that particular Greek word. In the Greek it has reference to enslaving power, setting forth the fact that the old man has not been annihilated, but crucified; its power has been "annulled," "put down," "made without effect."

This same Greek word *(katargethe)* is used in Hebrews 2:14, where at the cross our Lord is said to have "destroyed" the devil. Rather, it is there that He broke the enemy's power — he certainly was not annihilated! In Romans 3:3 this word is translated "make without effect"; in 3:31, "make void"; in 7:2, "loosed"; and in 7:6, "delivered." Self has been crucified at Calvary so that it may be rendered powerless to enslave us; made without effect so that we may be delivered from the reign and tyranny of the indwelling principle of sin, that henceforth we should not have to serve sin.

Our King James Version has a tendency to lead one astray in the area of reckoning because of its failure to set forth our death with Christ in the *past tense*. In this Version, the present tense is used in connection with these truths: concerning self, "our old man *is* crucified with him"; and concerning the believer, "he that *is* dead is freed from sin," and "if we *be* dead with Christ" (Rom. 6:6-8).

The American Standard Version (1901), which is more accurate for study purposes, gives us the contrasting correction. In Romans 6:6, "our old man *was* crucified with him"; verse 7, "he that *hath died* is justified [released] from [the tyranny of] sin"; and verse 8, "if we *died* with Christ." Thus the ASV makes it possible for us to reckon aright. In both versions, Romans 6:11 calls us to reckon ourselves *dead* unto sin, but *alive* unto God. The ASV enables us to see and understand that we *have died* unto sin but are now *alive* in Christ. We are not dead, but very much *alive as new creations*.

The usual mistake made in reckoning is to stop at the wrong point. The purpose of reckoning is that we may abide in Christ, who is our life. The first half, "dead unto sin," is but the stepping stone into the Land. If we stop short there, we are stranded in midstream. True reckoning is to step out firmly, and keep on going. We have died to the old Adamic source, but have been resurrected and are now alive in the new Source. *Death was the means, life is the goal.*

Although we are not to halt at the first half of our reckoning, neither are we in any way to regard that step as a superficial one. There can be no effective reckoning upon our life in Christ until we are firmly established in the truth of our having died to the old. The steps to maturity cannot be skipped over. Spiritual growth comes by walking in the Spirit, and He establishes us in each successive realm in preparation for the next. We cannot rest in our risen Lord until we know we have been positionally released from Adam through death. Neither can we rest in the *process* of being experientially released from the domination of the Adamic life until we know and count upon the fact that we are already loosed positionally.

True reckoning has its ultimate emphasis on the life-side of the cross; we count upon our having died unto sin in order to count upon our being alive unto God. Since we are new creations in Christ, death is forever past; we were brought out of it in Him at His resurrection. As for the old man within, we continually reckon that source to have been crucified, so that it may be held daily in the place of death. *We reckon; the cross crucifies.*

Look carefully at Colossians 3:3 (KJV): "For ye are dead, and your life is hid with Christ in God." However, we are not dead, but alive. Neither is self dead, but judicially crucified. We have forever passed beyond death. The American Standard Version brings out the past tense: "For ye died, and your life is hid with Christ in God." All the difference in the world! Once we see that our death unto sin is in the past tense, completed, we are free to count ourselves *alive* unto God in Christ Jesus, and to *live* — in the present tense!

The principle of life out of death is pictured both in our public baptism and in the Lord's Supper. Actually, our water baptism is to be a testimony of our reckoning. We count ourselves to have been baptized into (placed in union with) the Lord Jesus by the Spirit, and therefore we died unto sin with Him, were buried with Him, and arose in Him (Rom. 6:3,4). The testimony of this reckoning is carried out in pictorial form by our being baptized in (placed in) water, which covers us in burial, from which we arise to "walk in newness of life." We are confessing that we died and were buried, as far as the old source of life is concerned, and now are risen as new creations to walk in the Spirit of life in Christ

Jesus. Water baptism, therefore, holds less than its full meaning to the believer until he has apprehended the identification truths.

Water baptism testifies to our position: we have died to the old life, and are alive in the new. The Lord's Supper sets forth our experience (condition): we are being conformed to His death, so that His life may be manifested. We do not *leave* the influence of the cross to live, but we continually receive the benefit of its emancipation for our walk in newness of life. To what are we testifying in receiving and assimilating the broken bread and the fruit of the vine? "For as often as ye eat this bread, and drink this cup, ye do shew *the Lord's death* till he come" (1 Cor. 11:26).

The testimony of our baptism is a once-for-all picture of our reckoning upon the finished work, and represents our *position*. The Lord's Supper is a continuous picture of our being conformed to His death, and has to do with our *condition*. We confess that we are continually participating in His death, via reckoning, that His resurrection life may be increasingly manifested in and through our mortal bodies.

41

Chapter 7

Romans Seven
Reckoning

If believers knew more fully the deliverance of the first part of Romans Seven, they would experience less of the defeat of the latter part! This vitally important chapter has to do mainly with *the principle of law*.

Positionally, in Christ, no believer is under law. "The law was given by Moses, but grace and truth came by Jesus Christ"; "For Christ is the end of the law for righteousness to every one that believeth" (John 1:17; Rom. 10:4). Conditionally, almost all believers are to some extent under the principle of law "as a rule of life." The all-too-general attitude is: I must love the Lord and others; I must maintain my testimony; I must witness and work for Him; I must resist self; I must stop this sinning. The feeling of constraint expressed in "I must" makes for Romans Seven defeat.

"The law is holy . . . just, and good" (Rom. 7:12). The purpose of God's law, both in command and principle, is to bring to light and cause us to face up to the fact of our sinfulness, weakness, and bondage. Its faithful ministry, negative though it be, is all-important. Law does not make us sinners; it is holy, and reveals to us that we are sinful. "By the law is the knowledge of sin" (Rom. 3:20).

Anything we seek to do, or keep from doing, in our own strength brings us under legal bondage. Any promises or vows we make to the Lord, any code of ethics or rules of conduct that we set up for ourselves or have placed upon us, are on the basis of law and therefore result in failure and ever-deepening enslavement. The principle of law applies to the self-life, and can produce nothing but self-righteousness. Thus, the law convicts of our need of life in Christ.

The years of struggle and failure we experience are not only to prepare us for liberation from the tyranny of the principle of sin, but from the bondage of the principle of law. We are brought not only to the release of Romans Six, but to the deliverance of Romans Seven. We exchange "the law of sin and death" for "the law of the Spirit of life in Christ Jesus" (Rom. 8:2).

We are given the key to the problem of law at the very door of Romans Seven: *"Know ye not, brethren, . . . how that the law hath dominion over a man as long as he liveth?"* (Rom. 7:1). Exactly! All through the years of defeat, we have been slowly learning that the harder we tried to live the Christian life the deeper we came under the dominion of the law of sin. We tried to "be," we tried to "do," and there was nothing but failure year in and year out.

"For when we were in the flesh, the motions of sin, which were by the law, did work in our members to bring forth fruit [works] *unto death"* (Rom. 7:5). As long as we depended on our own resources, all we produced was sin; we hungered for life, and brought forth death. But in the midst of our wretched attempts to be delivered from the "body of this death" (Rom. 7:24), our faithful Father was teaching us what we had to know for our freedom in Christ: self is our greatest enemy, Christ is our only hope. "For to me to live is Christ" (Phil. 1:21).

With Paul, we came to recognize an internal law: when

we would do good, evil was present with us. That is, we saw another law in our members, warring against the law of our mind, and bringing us into captivity to the law of sin which is in our members (Rom. 7:21,23). All this has been specifically designed by the Spirit to bring us finally to the blessed condition of defeat where we cry from the heart, "O wretched man that I am! who shall deliver me from the body of this death?" (Rom. 7:24). Victory is found only through our realization of defeat: "I thank God through Jesus Christ our Lord" (Rom. 7:25).

First, we learn that our having died in Christ on the cross gives us the ground for freedom from the power of sin. But unless we learn the answer to the bondage of the principle of law, we will be right back in the defeat of Romans Seven, no matter how hard we reckon. Law reveals sin and produces bondage. The answer to the principle of sin prepares us for the answer to the principle of law. Reckoning is the key to both, and both have to do with the death of the cross and our life in Christ. *"But now we have been discharged from the law, having died to that wherein we were held; so that we serve in newness of the spirit, and not in oldness of the letter"* (Rom. 7:6, ASV). As Paul tells us in verse 1, as long as we lived and walked in the self-life we were under the principle and dominion of law.

But thanks be to God, we not only died to the principle of sin in Christ on the cross, but there we also died to (out from the dominion of) the principle of law! Further, we were not only thereby freed from the "oldness of the letter," but were joined to Him in "newness of spirit." *"Wherefore, my brethren, ye also were made dead to the law through the body of Christ; that ye should be joined to another, even to him who was raised from the dead, that we might bring forth fruit unto God"* (Rom. 7:4, ASV).

Here again we must be reminded that the *power* for deliverance from the law does not reside in the fact that we have died unto it, but in our *relationship* to the risen Liberator. "Christ the power of God" (1 Cor. 1:24). Unless we clearly reckon upon our having died to the principle of law, we are constantly under the pall of failing to meet our spiritual obligations. On the other hand, when we rest in our risen Lord we are more aware of His sufficiency than we are of the claims of law upon us, and we are able to walk in the "liberty wherewith Christ hath made us free" (Gal. 5:1). "Come unto me, all ye that labor and are heavy laden, and I will give you rest" (Matt. 11:28).

Each of us has "died unto the law" (Gal. 2:19, ASV), we were "discharged from the law" (Rom. 7:6), and we are now "not under law" (Rom. 6:14). We are completely out of the realm of the principle and command of the law, and are forever on the ground of grace in our Lord Jesus Christ. "The law came in besides, that the trespass might abound; but where sin abounded, grace did abound more exceedingly: that, as sin reigned in death, even so might grace reign through righteousness unto eternal life through Jesus Christ our Lord" (Rom. 5:20,21, ASV).

The Spirit of Truth is not only explicit and thorough in presenting the truth, but He is also exact and painstaking in preparing our hungry hearts for the appropriation of it. Most of His spiritual work He accomplishes in our lives through natural means, such as our careful, dependent study coupled with the vicissitudes of everyday life. The bondage of the principle of law finally brings us to its goal — the death of the cross. Now we are able to understand that "I through the law died unto the law, that I might live unto God. I have been crucified with Christ; and it is no longer I [self] that live, but Christ [my new life] liveth in me [new creation]: and that life which I now live in the flesh [body] I live in faith, the faith which is in the Son of God, who loved me, and gave himself up for me" (Gal. 2:19,20, ASV).

As we reckon upon having died to the principle of law, and abide in our risen Lord, the Holy Spirit progressively carries out the will of the Father in our life. His perfect will becomes a *delight* to us, not a *duty*. "For what the law could not do, in that it was weak through the flesh, God, sending his own Son in the likeness of sinful flesh and for sin, condemned sin in the flesh; that the ordinance of the law might be fulfilled in us, who walk not after the flesh, but after the Spirit" (Rom. 8:3,4, ASV), "not after the law of a carnal commandment, but after the power of an endless life" (Heb. 7:16).

"Stand fast therefore in the liberty wherewith Christ hath made us free, and be not entangled again with the yoke of bondage" (Gal. 5:1); "for the law of the Spirit of life in Christ Jesus hath made me free from the law of sin and death" (Rom. 8:2). "Reckon ye also yourselves to be dead unto sin [and law], but alive unto God in Christ Jesus" (Rom. 6:11, ASV).

Chapter 8

Romans Eight
Reckoning

There is a Spirit-fostered hunger and longing in the heart of every growing Christian for *the heaven-on-earth walk of Romans Eight.* The very purpose of reckoning is that we may live in this wonderful — and practical — realm of life in Christ. All that the Holy Spirit teaches us in Romans Six, and takes us through in Romans Seven, combines to prepare us for the walk of Romans Eight. This, in turn, brings us on to the blessed heights of Ephesians and Colossians.

Through the years, whether we realize it or not, the Holy Spirit is developing us "from glory to glory" (2 Cor. 3:18) along His prescribed path. Romans Six is the *step* that deals with the principle of sin, and is the answer to its power. Romans Seven is the *struggle* (usually years in duration) that has to do with the principle of law, and brings the answer to its bondage. Romans Eight is the *walk* based on the principle of life in Christ as ministered by the Spirit of Life.

In studying some of the truths of this heart-satisfying eighth chapter of Romans, we must once more give special attention to the very first verse. This is another instance where the King James Version might lead us into bondage, unless we study with care. "There is therefore now no condemnation to them which are in Christ Jesus, who walk not after the flesh, but after the Spirit" (vs. 1). This text is actually stating that there is no condemnation for us *if* we do not walk after the flesh, and *if* we walk after the Spirit. Thus, our eternal safety would depend upon our present walk; this is law, rather than grace.

We can praise the Lord that the entire New Testament teaches differently — that we escape condemnation through our eternal position in Christ, not our present condition in ourselves. Once more we apply to the corrected American Standard Version: *"There is therefore now no condemnation to them that are in Christ Jesus."* We are free solely because of our redemption and position in Christ, apart from "conditions." The remainder of the King James Version's verse (the conditions), belongs in verse 4 of this chapter and has to do with something else, as we shall see later.

Notice how correctly and powerfully the truth is now revealed, as these first two verses fit together without the erroneous interpolation. "There is therefore now no condemnation to them that are in Christ Jesus. For the law of the Spirit of life in Christ Jesus made me free from the law of sin and of death" (Rom. 8:1,2, ASV).

There is actually a dual application in the truth of Romans 8:1 and 2. Concerning the future, the law of the Spirit of life in Christ has freed us from the eternal condemnation of the law of sin and death. As to the present, the Holy Spirit ministers the *life* of the Lord Jesus within for our daily walk, progressively freeing us from the power of sin and the deathly influence it spawns. "For if while we were enemies we were reconciled to God through the death of His Son, it is much more (certain), now that we are reconciled, that we shall be saved (daily delivered from sin's dominion) through His (resurrection) *life*" (Rom. 5:10, Amp.). We are saved from the condemnation of sin because of His reconciliation;

we are delivered from the power of sin because of His *life*.

Especially in our early years as believers, most of us have felt that it was our responsibility, with the Lord's help, to live the Christian life. Our unqualified failure in attempting to do so has been the Holy Spirit's means of showing us that we cannot "produce," nor are we meant to. Only the Lord Jesus can live His life through us; and He does this as we reject our own resources, to walk in reliance upon the Spirit of Life. "That the righteousness of the law might be fulfilled in us, who walk not after the flesh, but after the Spirit" (Rom. 8:4). This is the addition we noted in verse 1 of the King James Version. It belongs here as verse 4, not having to do with our redemption or condemnation, but with our walk and growth.

What it takes years for us to learn thoroughly is that the Holy Spirit ministers *all*. By the Spirit we are sealed, we live, we grow, and we shall be raised (Eph. 1:13; Rom. 8:10; 2 Cor. 3:8; Rom. 8:11). It is especially important for us that He is the *Spirit of Life*. Even though we are alive in Christ Jesus, we have no power by which to live the new life; for that, as well as for everything else, we must rely upon the Holy Spirit. (Incidentally, He should not be referred to as the "Holy Ghost.")

Too many Christians today are seeking to live for the Lord on the basis of *the principle of love*. Their thinking is, "He loved me and gave Himself for me, therefore the least I can do is love Him and give myself to Him." Such a motive is good, high, and altruistic; but it is neither the best nor the highest, nor is it spiritual. Our love is far too weak and vacillating for such an undertaking. *Self* will see to that! "For to will is present with me; but how to perform that which is good I find not . . . . For I delight in the law of God after the inward man. But I see another law in my members . . . bringing me into captivity to the law of sin" (Rom. 7:18,22,23).

There is only one true and adequate *motivating power* for living the Christian life, and that is the very life of the Lord Jesus — ministered within by the Spirit of Life Himself. This is not a motivation of love, but the *empowerment of life*. "For to me to live is Christ" (Phil. 1:21). It is not, "Only what is done *for* Christ will last," but rather, "Only what is done *by* Christ will last."

In Romans 8:6 we must again take a close look at our King James Version: "For to be carnally minded is death; but to be spiritually minded is life and peace." This particular translation runs counter to the actual teaching of the Word. For the believer to be "carnally minded" does not bring death, as all believers pass through a great deal of carnality as part of their growth. To be "spiritually minded" does not bring life, as all believers are alive in Christ.

Once more, the American Standard Version states the truth accurately: "For the mind of the flesh is death; but the mind of the Spirit is life and peace" (Rom. 8:6). Here, the Word is stating that the make-up, the bent, the life of the flesh, is nothing but death; whereas that of the Spirit is life and peace — the life of Christ, and the peace of God. Verse 7 further reveals the nature of the flesh: "Because the mind of the flesh is enmity against God; for it is not subject to the law of God, neither indeed can it be."

The flesh in its entirety, all of self, is dead set against God and everything spiritual. "In my flesh dwelleth no good thing" (Rom. 7:18). The flesh is at absolute enmity with

50

God, and can neither be reconciled nor redeemed. It took the death of the Son and our newly created life in Him to bring us to God. Our old source was not changed, but crucified; it was exchanged for the new creation in Christ Jesus. "For they that are in the flesh cannot please God" (Rom. 8:8).

We exchanged the position of death for the position of life. By means of our identification in the Lord Jesus on the cross, we were "cut out of the olive tree which is wild by nature [Adam]," and were "grafted contrary to nature into a good olive tree [Christ]" (Rom. 11:24). How glorious to be a newly created branch grafted into the True Vine!

As the life of the Vine flows by the Spirit of Life, the fruit of the Spirit is increasingly manifested in the branch: "love, joy, peace, longsuffering, gentleness, goodness, faith, meekness, temperance: against such there is no law" (Gal. 5:22,23). In the Vine, we are complete; in ourselves, we are being "completed" through the growth based on reckoning. We are gradually being conformed to the image of our Lord Jesus Christ (Rom. 8:29).

the Flesh = us — our whole being
my
all of me as I am in Adam

the spirit = me — my whole being
all of me as I am in Christ

Chapter 9

The Self-life and Reckoning

To be perfectly scriptural, it must be said that the reckoning of Romans 6:11 has nothing whatsoever to do with the self-life. We are certainly not to reckon the old man to have "died unto sin," any more than we are to reckon him to be "alive unto God in Christ." The reckoning of this key verse applies to the "new creation in Christ Jesus."

It is as a "new man" in Christ that I am to reckon myself to have died unto the principle of sin, and to be alive unto God in Christ Jesus. While God knew me as a lost individual in Adam, He also foreknew me as a believer in Christ. At Calvary, He not only identified the Lord Jesus with my sins by making Him "to be sin for us" (2 Cor. 5:21), but He also identified me, the sinner, with the Lord Jesus. As Redeemer, He died there in payment *for* the penalty of my sins; as Life, He died *unto* (out from the jurisdiction of) sin. In my identification with Him, the death of the cross separated me from the power and tyranny of the principle of sin.

As Life, and having fully paid the penalty of our sins, the Lord Jesus arose from among the dead. Being identified with Christ, I, as an individual cut off from sinful Adam, was created anew in Him. Romans 6:11 calls upon me, as a new creation in Christ, to reckon myself alive unto God in Him, having died unto sin at Calvary. By faith in these facts, I am to rest in my eternal position — alive in the risen Lord —

looking upon the death of the cross as separating me from the influence of sin and self.

I am a new creation in the Last Adam. Judicially, the old things of the first Adam have passed away, both as to their penalty and their power. "The first man is of the earth, earthy; the second man is the Lord from heaven. . . . And as we have borne the image of the earthy, we shall also bear the image of the heavenly" (1 Cor. 15:47,49). My history in the earthy Adam having been brought to an end at Calvary, I now count upon my relationship to the heavenly Adam to conform me to His image.

Our reckoning has to do with our position in Christ, not our condition in the body. Although the Adamic life is not the source of my Christian life, that source is still active in my mortal body. When I fail to reckon upon, and abide in, the Lord Jesus as my new life, the old life expresses itself by "the works of the flesh" in my members. Paul's alternative to this is, "Neither present your members unto sin as instruments of unrighteousness; but present yourselves unto God, *as alive from the dead*, and your members as instruments of right-eousness unto God" (Rom. 6:13, ASV). When we yield to sin and the old life, the result is unrighteousness; when we yield our "alive-from-the-dead" life unto God, there is right-eousness. "I beseech you therefore, brethren, by the mercies of God, that ye present your bodies a living sacrifice . . . unto God" (Rom. 12:1).

"But thanks be to God, that, whereas ye were servants of sin, ye became obedient from the heart to that form of teaching [identification] whereunto ye were delivered; and being made free from [the tyranny of] sin, ye became servants of righteousness. . . . But now being made free from [the power of] sin and become servants to God, ye have your fruit [of the Spirit] unto sanctification" (Rom. 6:17,18,22, ASV). In reckoning, we are thereby yielding ourselves to our risen Lord, and the fruit of His life is manifested in us by growth in His image. When we fail to count upon His life, the old Adamic source exercises its sinful influence and power throughout our being, making us carnal, self-centered believers.

Romans 6:6 (ASV) affirms that the Adamic source of life within was crucified on the cross: "Knowing this, that our old man was crucified with him." We may have tried for years in our Romans Seven struggles to overcome and crucify self, but there was only miserable failure. Now we finally stop struggling, and begin to trust. We reckon upon what was done with that source on Calvary, thereby enabling the law of the Spirit of life in Christ Jesus to free us from the law of sin and death.

When we have sinned, or are about to be overcome by the old man, it is *too late* then to reckon. No, our reckoning concerning self is to become our *heart-attitude*. We know that the old source was crucified at the cross, and we continually count on that fact — it is to be the set of our mind. We begin the day in that attitude of heart; we do not wait until a need arises. In this way, the influence of the cross is more consistently applied to self, and our resultant emancipation becomes progressively confirmed.

"Christ suffered in the flesh — for us, was crucified for our sin. Therefore arm yourselves with the same purpose (to suffer rather than to sin), for he whose mortal nature has suffered (in Christ's Person and been crucified) has done with sin — has obtained a ceasing from (the domination of) sin.

54

So that he can no longer spend the rest of his natural life living by (his) human appetites and desires, but (he lives) for what God wills" (1 Pet. 4:1,2, Amp.). In reckoning, our attitude becomes one of a firm stand against self, cost what it may. *The price of birth is His death for us; the price of growth is our death with Him.* ✳

It is difficult for us to realize and acquiesce to the fact that *suffering* is one of the main factors in our spiritual growth. In the first place, we are in union of life with a suffering Savior whose earthly ministry was expressed in sacrifice for others. Secondly, there is the suffering we go through when we fail to abide in Him, but walk in the flesh — the suffering of sin and its inevitable consequences. Thirdly, there is the suffering that results from our day-by-day emancipation from the influence of the self-life by means of crucifixion.

Our *hatred of self* is actually developed and strengthened during our miserable years of slavery to it. We never realize the necessity and value of Romans Seven failure while we are in its throes. It is normal and healthy to begin the Christian life victoriously, but in those infant days we know little or nothing about self, and little enough of the Lord Jesus. To rectify this deficiency, the Holy Spirit reveals the carnality of self — that we may ultimately grow into the maturity of Christ.

Through this practical revelation of the sinfulness of self we gain the knowledge of the holiness of Christ, and our need for counting upon Him as our life. Until we thoroughly hate and distrust self, we are not fully able to love and trust the Lord Jesus. Conversely, the more we grow to love Him, the more clearly do we see self for what it is. All through our earthly life, the Holy Spirit will be allowing us to get into situations where we will discover ever deeper manifestations of the old source. For this reason He develops within us the proper "mind" — the mind to *suffer* in the flesh, rather than *yield* to the flesh.

This is the heart-attitude we, as believers, need today. Many of us willingly reckon upon the crucifixion of the old man, only to draw back from the cross when we feel the bite of the nails. It takes a real *hatred* of the old life, coupled with a deep *hunger* for the new, to be able to glory in the cross that crucifies.

But when we stand firm in the Lord Jesus, armed with a mind to suffer rather than sin, then it is we are yielded and willing to be "alway delivered unto death for Jesus' sake, that the life also of Jesus might be made manifest in our mortal flesh" (2 Cor. 4:11). We realize that the practical crucifixion of the cross is freeing us from the life hated by both God and us, and all that matters is that the life of the Lord Jesus may be seen in and through us. "So then death worketh in us, but life in you" (2 Cor. 4:12). "Wherefore let them that suffer according to the will of God commit the keeping of their souls to him in well-doing, as unto a faithful Creator" (1 Pet. 4:19).

Chapter 10

Reckoning in Galatians 2:20

Nowhere does the believer go farther astray than by *reckoning self dead!* For, if the old man died at the cross, it would mean he was annihilated. To reckon self to be dead results in the error of eradication. But every honest Christian knows only too well that the self-life is very much alive within. To err is to cut the lifeline to healthy spiritual development.

On the other hand, we are to view the old man as having been *crucified*: nailed to the cross, helpless, but not *slain*. (See Chapter 6.) "Our old man was crucified with him, that the body of sin [the law of sin in our members] might be '*katargethe*' " (Rom. 6:6). This Greek word carries these meanings: "held inoperative," "annulled," "made without effect," "power broken," "put down."

As we reckon upon that crucifixion, the Holy Spirit applies the effect of the cross to self, holding it inoperative and thereby freeing us from its power. Our failure to reckon will release the old man from the cross to resume his sinful reign in our members. There could not be this resumption if self were dead.

Galatians 2:20 (ASV) clearly delineates the two sources of life involved in our reckoning: "I have been crucified with Christ; and it is no longer I that live, but Christ liveth in me: and that life which I now live in the flesh I live in faith, the faith which is in the Son of God, who loved me, and gave himself up for me." How important it is diligently to "study . . . rightly dividing the Word of truth" (2 Tim. 2:15). Unless *the principle of distinctions* is faithfully adhered to, our reckoning will be invalid and come to nought.

"I have been crucified with Christ." The identity of this "I" is clearly disclosed in Romans 6:6: "Our old man was crucified with him." Our sinful, Adamic source of life was crucified in Christ on Calvary. In our daily walk this self-life is not slain, but crucified — held in the place of death, rendered inoperative by the work of the cross.

"And it is no longer I that live." "I" as the old creation, my history in Adam, ended at the cross. For me as a new creation in Christ, the death of the cross constitutes full separation from the reign of the old life.

"But Christ liveth in me." This refers to "me" as newly created in the risen Lord. "I am the Vine, ye are the branches: he that abideth in me, and I in him . . ." (John 15:5). When our Father identified each of us with the Lord Jesus on the cross, all the life that came from the fallen Adam source was crucified; we, as individuals, were taken down into His death and raised as new creations in Christ. "For if we have become united with him in the likeness of his death, we shall be also in the likeness of his resurrection" (Rom. 6:5, ASV).

Think for a moment of 2 Corinthians 5:17: "If any man be in Christ, he is a new creature [creation]: old things are passed away; behold, all things are become new." This speaks of our *position*, not our *condition*. Our condition will develop from this completed position by means of our reckoning faith. When we arose from the dead in Christ, we were created anew, cut off from the old source of life by the cross and joined to the new Source in the "power of an endless life." "Old things are passed away": the old man is passed away, as far as the new life is concerned — separated by the death of Calvary. "All things are become new": everything is new in Christ, for we are a completely new creation. It is not that the old life is changed, but crucified, and exchanged for the new life.

"*And that life which I now live in the flesh* [*body*] *I live in faith.*" This is the newly created "I" as a born-again believer in Christ risen; and I now live by faith. "*The faith which is in the Son of God.*" I count upon Him, not upon self. "*Who loved me and gave himself up for me.*" The Lord Jesus did not love the old man; He took him to the cross! I am also to hate my (old) life, and count it a crucified thing held in the place of death by the Holy Spirit. The Lord Jesus loves the new "me," the branch in the True Vine.

The subject of our reckoning may be further clarified by separating *the three parts of the one heart-attitude*:

(1) Identified with Christ, "we have become united with him in the likeness of his death" (Rom. 6:5, ASV). We were spiritually baptized into His death by virtue of being identified with Him. "Know ye not, that so many of us as were baptized into Jesus Christ were baptized into his death?" (Rom. 6:3). This has reference to the true baptism of the Spirit. "For by one Spirit are we all baptized into one body" (1 Cor. 12:13). Water baptism by immersion is a pictorial testimony of this finished work. Knowing ourselves to have been identified with Christ, we are able to reckon ourselves to have died unto sin.

(2) Reckoning that we died at the cross in Christ is not

reckoning ourselves to be dead now. We passed *through* death, and are forever alive as new creations in Him. God "hath quickened [enlifed, re-created] us together, with Christ . . . and hath raised us up together, and made us sit together in heavenly places in Christ Jesus" (Eph. 2:5,6). Being brought out of death in His resurrection gives us ground upon which to reckon ourselves alive unto God in Christ.

(3) As for the Adamic "law of sin which is in my members," we reckon upon the fact that it has been crucified (not "destroyed"), its power over us as new creations "broken," and "rendered void." As we reckon upon this truth, the Holy Spirit applies the crucifixion of the cross to self, and we are progressively freed from its influence while walking in dependence upon the Spirit. If we become careless, or choose to walk in the flesh and draw from the resources of self, the old man is at once free to bring forth "the works of the flesh" in our members. But as we increase in knowledge of the finished work, and allow the cross to separate us in experience from the Adamic source while the Spirit develops the new life within us, we grow in the "not I, but Christ" walk.

There is further light on *the principle of distinctions* in Romans 7:19 and 20. Here, the mighty Paul is learning that in his own strength he is powerless against the indwelling law of sin. "For the good that I would I do not: but the evil which I would not, that I do. Now if I do that I would not, it is no more I that do it, but sin that dwelleth in me." Note the distinction between the two sources within — sins flowing from the old source, not the new. He also discovers that even as a new creation in Christ, he cannot by his own endeavors overcome indwelling sin.

The fallen Adam life within, the very embodiment of the principle of sin, can do nothing but sin. "For I know that in me (that is, in my flesh) dwelleth no good thing" (Rom. 7:18). The Last Adam, the very life of Christ within, cannot sin, and is manifested as "the fruit of the Spirit." "Whosoever is born of God doth not commit sin . . . and he cannot sin, because he is born of God" (1 John 3:9). As we reckon upon the crucifixion of the *first Adam* source, the flow of indwelling sin is progressively cut off by the daily work of the cross. And while we reckon upon our new life in the *Last Adam*, the flow of His endless life is increasingly deepened by the Spirit of life in Christ Jesus.

The source of our Christian life is distinctly revealed in Romans 8:9: "But ye are not in the flesh, but in the Spirit, if so be that the Spirit of God dwell in you. Now if any man have not the Spirit of Christ [the Holy Spirit], he is none of his." God sees us as *"not in the flesh, but in the Spirit."* We are to reckon likewise. As individuals identified with the Lord Jesus, we were cut off from fallen Adam in His death, and created anew in Him in His resurrection. The source of our new life is the Last Adam, who indwells us by the Holy Spirit. This is *the principle of the two Adams (sources).*

Although as believers we are "not in the flesh, but in the Spirit," the self-life will flow (and grow) as long as we fail to reckon upon the work of the cross, and to abide in Christ. Contrariwise, as we walk in dependence upon the Spirit, He will cause the indwelling life of the Lord Jesus to flow through us as "rivers of living water."

There is the allegory of the sea captain who, in mid-ocean, is charged with a capital offense, put in chains, and replaced by another. As the ship sails on, the chained one

61

seeks to assert his old authority over the crew. Some of them might be foolish enough to respond, but there is no need to for he has been judicially deposed. It is now simply a matter of acknowledging the new captain, and refusing the threats and orders of the condemned one. The death sentence is not yet carried out beyond his being held in the place of death, his power broken, but he will be executed when the ship reaches port. In the meantime, he causes a lot of trouble.

Is this not a picture of the Adamic source, held in the place of death, replaced by the new Source at the helm of our ship? Our attitude toward the old man is to be this: "I reckon upon the crucifixion of the cross as your undoing, and therefore refuse your reign over me. I count the Lord Jesus Christ as the Captain of my life." When we reach the heavenly port, the conflict will be over; in the meantime, we rest in Him.

Chapter 11

Reckoning in Philippians 3:10

Philippians 3:10 involves reckoning. It is often quoted but seldom understood. It sets forth first the Christian's *goal*, then the means and process by which that goal is reached: "That I may know him, and the power of his resurrection, and the fellowship of his sufferings, being made conformable unto his death."

"That I may know him." The one reason for our existence as believers is to come to know the Lord Jesus Christ; and it is through this knowledge that we know our heavenly Father. Let it be repeated, and may it be heeded: "This is life eternal, that they might *know* thee the only true God, and Jesus Christ, whom thou hast sent" (John 17:3). This is to be personal, oneness-of-nature knowledge, not just knowledge *about* Him. Entering into this wonderful fellowship of union with Him is going to require the best of our attention here, and all of it in eternity.

The key to knowing the Lord Jesus here and now is the Word of God. We can learn about Him through our general study of the Scriptures, but we can only get to know Him personally by *feeding* upon Him therein. In our devotions, we should concentrate on the Living Word as revealed in the written Word. In this quiet fellowship, we study Him in Scripture in dependence upon the Spirit of Truth. We get to know Him as we meditate upon Him in the Word, both as

He was on earth and as He is in glory — observing His character (attitudes, actions and reactions), listening to Him speak, speaking to Him, responding to Him, loving and trusting Him.

While we feed upon Christ as the Bread of Life, and abide in Him as the True Vine, the faithful Holy Spirit is forming Him deep within the springs of our life, within our very spirit where He abides. Gazing upon the Lord Jesus in the authoritative Word keeps us under the transforming influence of *the principle of assimilation*: "We all, with open face beholding as in a glass the glory of the Lord, are changed into the same image from glory to glory, even as by the Spirit of the Lord" (2 Cor. 3:18).

"The power of His resurrection." We first know this mighty power of His resurrection and ascension when we see our scriptural *position* in our risen Lord. The foundation of all resurrection life is death. "For if we have been planted together in the likeness of his death, we shall be also in the likeness of his resurrection" (Rom. 6:5). "But God, who is rich in mercy, for his great love wherewith he loved us . . . hath quickened us together with Christ . . . and hath raised us up together" (Eph. 2:4-6). We are new creations in Christ Jesus by the power of His resurrection.

Our reckoning is to be based upon our *position*. We count ourselves alive unto God in Christ. Through our faith in this fact, the Holy Spirit makes this truth real in our *condition*, our growth. We abide in Him above, and He manifests Himself in us below. In reckoning, we are yielding; our faith rests upon the fact that God has raised us together with the Lord Jesus, and this enables us to yield ourselves unto God *"as those that are alive from the dead"* (Rom. 6:13).

64

We abide in Him above,
He manifests Himself
in us below

Certainly, we cannot yield ourselves to God when we do not know we are *free* to do so. We are hopelessly taken up with the struggle for freedom, unless we are aware we have been cut off from the slavery of sin and self through our having died on the cross. Until we know we are alive from the dead, we cannot yield to Him as such. We do not yield to become free, but *because* we are free in the risen Lord. Having died unto the old, we are alive and free in the new. Count it so.

Finally, we will know the power of His resurrection when our physical bodies are changed, at the Lord's return. "If the Spirit of him that raised up Jesus from the dead dwell in you, he that raised up Christ from the dead shall also quicken your mortal bodies by his Spirit that dwelleth in you" (Rom. 8:11). "For our citizenship is in heaven; whence also we wait for a Saviour, the Lord Jesus Christ: who shall fashion anew the body of our humiliation, that it may be conformed to the body of his glory, according to the working whereby he is able even to subject all things unto himself. Wherefore, my brethren beloved and longed for, my joy and crown, so stand fast in the Lord" (Phil. 3:20,21; 4:1, ASV).

We know the power of His resurrection in our position; we are realizing that power in our spiritual growth; we will forever know His mighty power in our resurrection bodies. "When Christ, who is our life, shall appear, then shall ye also appear with him in glory" (Col. 3:4).

"The fellowship of His sufferings." Suffering is the lot of all men, the privilege of all believers. The general thinking is that God is not blessing unless He keeps us from, or relieves us of, suffering. Far from it! There is no fellowship with, and

65

growth in, the crucified Lord without suffering — physical, mental, and spiritual.

Fellowship with the Lord Jesus Christ is the source of our suffering. "If, when ye do well, and suffer for it, ye take it patiently, this is acceptable with God. For even hereunto were ye called: because Christ also suffered for us, leaving us an example, that ye should follow his steps" (1 Pet. 2:20,21). Paul is our *pattern* of suffering as a Christian. As soon as the apostle was saved, the Lord Jesus said, "I will shew him how great things he must suffer for my name's sake" (Acts 9:16). "Alway delivered unto death for Jesus' sake" (2 Cor. 4:11). Paul's sufferings (see 2 Cor. 11:23-28, for instance) came indirectly from the nail-pierced hands and spear-pierced heart of his Lord. *All* these things were working together for his good. Notice Paul's attitude! "I obtained *mercy*, that in me first Jesus Christ might shew forth all longsuffering, for a pattern to them which should afterward believe on him to life everlasting" (1 Tim. 1:16). "If so be that we suffer with him, that we may be also glorified together. For I reckon that the sufferings of this present time are not worthy to be compared with the *glory* which shall be revealed in us" (Rom. 8:17,18). "If we suffer, we shall also *reign* with him" (2 Tim. 2:12).

Our fellowship in His sufferings bears threefold fruit. In suffering we *learn something of the process of growth*. "Knowing that tribulation worketh patience; and patience, experience" (Rom. 5:3,4). He chastens (child-trains) us "for our profit, that we might be partakers of his holiness" (Heb. 12:10). In suffering we also *learn more of Him*. "For as the sufferings of Christ abound in us, so our consolation also aboundeth by Christ" (2 Cor. 1:5). And in suffering we *learn to appreciate the needs of others.* "Blessed be God . . . the God of all comfort; who comforteth us in all our tribulation, that we may be able to comfort them which are in any trouble, by the comfort wherewith we ourselves are comforted of God" (2 Cor. 1:3,4).

"Being made conformable unto his death." We are "alway delivered unto death for Jesus' sake," and thereby are being "conformed to his death" — that we may be conformed to His image. As we take up our cross daily, this conformation is worked out in the two aspects of *death* and *life*. Self is dealt with by the crucifixion of Calvary; its power is broken by the death process within. As a result, the crucified life of the Lord Jesus is manifested in our mortal bodies. "Let this mind [attitude] be in you, which was also in Christ Jesus: who . . . made himself of no reputation, and took upon him the form of a servant . . . and being found in fashion as a man, he humbled himself, and became obedient unto death, even the death of the cross" (Phil. 2:5,7,8).

As we remain within the crucifying influence of the cross, we are freed to abide in the life-giving influence of the Resurrected One. We are to be conformed to His death as the basis of our being conformed to the image of His life-out-of-death. In this alien world we are as pilgrims, crucified followers of our crucified Lord. "He said to them all, If any man will come after me, let him deny himself, and take up his cross daily, and follow me" (Luke 9:23).

Chapter 12

Reckoning in
Colossians Three

The first valid faith we exercised toward God was by means of reckoning. We counted upon the Lord Jesus as our personal Savior, and were thereby saved. *The principle of reckoning* is to have faith in a *finished work*. Nowhere is this principle more explicitly revealed than in Colossians Three.

"If [since] then ye were raised together with Christ, seek the things that are above, where Christ is, seated on the right hand of God. Set your mind on the things that are above, not on the things that are upon the earth. For ye died, and your life is hid with Christ in God. When Christ, who is our life, shall be manifested, then shall ye also with him be manifested in glory" (Col. 3:1-4, ASV).

"If [since] then ye were raised together with Christ." Here, as always, Paul sets forth the doctrine before he presents the exhortation. He does likewise in Ephesians, revealing the wonderful fact that God "hath raised us up together, and made us sit together in heavenly places in Christ Jesus" (Eph. 2:6). This is the truth we need in order to reckon, so that we may abide in Him above and He may be manifested in us here below.

"Seek the things that are above, where Christ is, seated on the right hand of God." Reckoning ourselves alive unto God in Christ amounts to our taking our position in Him. Since the heavenly sphere is now our true position, it follows that

we are to seek there the things of Christ — spiritual realities. Everything in heaven is centered in Christ, "For in him dwelleth all the fulness of the Godhead bodily. And ye are complete in him" (Col. 2:9,10).

Our Father yearns for fellowship with His own. How can His heart-longing be satisfied apart from our feeding on the things of Christ, so that we may enter into oneness of mind and purpose with Him? To this end we have been made partakers of the divine nature.

Although we seek, and learn, *from* our risen position, yet the revelation comes *through* the Word. All, all depends upon our knowledge of the scriptural facts. Through our Spirit-taught study of God's Word, we are given both the revelation of the truth, and its practical reality in our lives.

"Set your mind on the things that are above, not on the things that are upon the earth." As we "eat of the old corn of the land" (Josh. 5:11), feeding upon the Lord Jesus in heaven by means of the Word, we learn of Him and grow in Him. Our mind is set upon the One in whom we live, not upon self and this world unto which we have died. "For where your treasure is, there will your heart be also" (Luke 12:34).

Dr. C. I. Scofield comments on Joshua 5:11 as follows: "The manna is a type of Christ in humiliation, known 'after the flesh,' giving His flesh that the believer might have life (John 6:49-51); while the *'old corn of the land'* is Christ apprehended as risen, glorified, and seated in the heavenlies. Occupation with Christ on earth, 'crucified through weakness,' tends to a wilderness experience. An experience befitting the believer's place in the heavenlies demands an apprehension of the power of His resurrection (2 Cor. 5:16; 13:4; Phil. 3:10; Eph. 1:15-23). It is the contrast between 'milk' and 'meat' in Paul's writings (1 Cor. 3:1,2; Heb. 5:12-14; 6:1-3)."

The Holy Spirit ministers life exclusively from the true, heavenly Source, Christ. He is the Spirit of Christ, and He gives us the things of the glorified Lord. Even so, if we fail to reckon upon our having died unto sin at Calvary, the old earthy source within will continue to produce its stream of carnality. As our mind is set on things that are upon the earth, we become increasingly earth-bound and self-centered. When we set our minds upon Christ and abide in Him as our risen life, we become increasingly conformed to His image.

"For ye died, and your life is hid with Christ in God." In this one brief statement Paul compresses the entire finished work of Romans Six, the whole truth of our identification with Christ. Upon these twelve one-syllable words our reckoning for growth is founded!

In this concise statement, Paul is dealing mainly with our relationship to the world and things earthly. Our having died on Calvary not only separated us from the reign of sin and self, but also from the deadly influence of this present world. By means of the cross "the world is crucified unto me, and I unto the world" (Gal. 6:14).

"For ye died." The only way we can escape the influence of the earthly sphere, the very element in which the self-life thrives, is to count upon our having died unto it. The death through which we passed now stands between us and the world.

"And your life is hid with Christ in God." Our Father not only has cut us off from the world system, but He has hidden us from its deadly power. We are in it, but not of it. Our life is

anchored in, and maintained by, our risen Lord Jesus. The reason so many Christians are not living *from* their heavenly position in the Liberator is that they are not yet established in the truth of their freedom from the influence of the world.

There is a continuity of reckoning that must be followed; no step can be by-passed. Until we know and reckon upon the truth of our having died *out of* the Adamic creation, we cannot exercise intelligent faith in counting that: (1) we are a new creation in Christ Jesus; (2) we are alive unto God in Him; (3) our life is hid with Christ in God. Established positionally, we will become established experientially.

When we learn to fix our mind upon Christ and rest in Him in the heavenlies, we will not be oppressed by self, circumstances, and situations here on earth. Our spiritual position is not down here, praying and pleading for help from Him up there. Just the opposite! We do not go *to* Him for help, but we rest *in* Him as the All-sufficient One. We do not bring Him down to our level for our use; we abide in Him at His level, for His use.

"When Christ, who is our life, shall be manifested, then shall ye also with Him be manifested in glory." Christ is our Christian life; therefore, as we grow spiritually we become more like Him. At His second coming, we shall even have a glorious body like His. Our Father has already glorified us in Christ; our Lord's return will bring the manifestation of that finished work. "And whom he justified, them he also glorified" (Rom. 8:30). Count and rest upon it. "For our citizenship is in heaven; whence also we wait for a Saviour, the Lord Jesus Christ: who shall fashion anew the body of our humiliation, that it may be conformed to the body of his glory" (Phil. 3:21, ASV).

71

"Ye have put off the old man" (Col. 3:9). When was this accomplished? At Calvary! There we were separated from the old by our death in Christ. Now, experientially, we are cut off from the doings of the old man by reckoning upon his crucifixion.

"And have put on the new man, which is renewed in knowledge after the image of him that created him" (Col. 3:10). The new man was put on when we were re-created in the Lord Jesus. This new nature is the very life of the One who is the express image of God. Therefore, our growth in the knowledge of Him results in the manifestation of His life.

For years we try to handle the problem of sin and self *directly*. On the negative side, we seek to suppress self, or crucify the old nature. On the positive side, we plead with God to change us for the better, and we try to be more Christlike. But in it all, we never seem to emerge from Romans Seven — total defeat.

Finally, we learn to meet the problem *indirectly*, by reckoning. We see in the Word that the old man has been effectively "put off" at the cross; and we also see that the new man has been "put on" through our resurrection in Christ. Instead of being taken up with the problem, we now set our mind and heart on God's answer: the crucifying cross and the risen Christ.

Chapter 13

The Rest of Reckoning

"Leaving the doctrine of the first principles of Christ, let us press on unto perfection [full growth]" (Heb. 6:1, ASV). As hungry and growing believers, we press on — but we do not press to "produce." The Holy Spirit instills within our being a determination that will not be denied, a hunger that must be satisfied. Our pressing on to His very best is fostered by the fact that we will never be satisfied in ourselves, but we will always be satisfied in Him. We are ever being drawn forward because of our realized need for freedom and growth. "This one thing I do, forgetting those things which are behind, and reaching forth unto those things which are before, I press toward the mark for the prize of the high calling of God in Christ Jesus" (Phil. 3:13,14).

Thank God for our needs! They are the primary impetus toward His abundant life. Remember the wretchedness, agony, and frustration we knew, with very little hope or assurance that things would ever improve? We were overwhelmed by problems, and not yet aware of His answer to them. But we continued on in desperation, for deep within our spirit there was the constant yearning for freedom from struggle, and *rest in His life*. Our striving ebbed and flowed, but there was never a moment of rest. During our enslavement by sin and self, the faithful indwelling Spirit did not let us give up.

When the Holy Spirit has brought us into the depths of Romans Seven, we have learned enough about self to acknowledge that it brings forth nothing but death (Rom. 7:24). Then it is that the Spirit centers our attention anew upon the Lord Jesus, and we realize that He, not our futile struggling, has provided freedom from our bondage. "Who shall deliver me . . .? I thank God through Jesus Christ our Lord" (Rom. 7:24,25)! Thus, when our reliance is wrenched from self and every other broken reed, the Spirit has us prepared to *rest* upon the written Word and in the Living Word. By means of the identification truths, the Spirit shows us the finished work of the cross and our life in Christ, and we begin to *reckon*.

What a difference our new reliance upon the truth makes! We press on with more determination than ever, and with an even greater hunger for His best. But now, the wonderful contrast is that in the midst of our pressing on, there is *rest*; the struggle is gone. We have entered into His rest because we know the facts; we know our position of freedom through the cross, and life abundant in our risen Lord. Now we have the assurance that, as we reckon upon the truths, the Holy Spirit will cause us to grow in them daily. There is rest in the midst of growth.

The Word presents an interesting paradox concerning this rest. "There remaineth therefore a rest to the people of God. For he that is entered into his rest, he also hath ceased from his own works, as God did from his. Let us *labor* therefore to enter into that *rest*" (Heb. 4:9-11). It is certain that there is no rest of faith as long as we struggle to "produce." And the hungry heart will not cease its striving until the truth of the finished work is seen and counted upon. This is *the principle of rest*, by which we were born in Him, and by which we grow in Him.

The actual "labor" mentioned in verse 11 has to do with believing. It is quite an exercise to reckon that we died unto sin and self, when we are keenly aware of their presence and manifestation in our life. It is also "labor" to believe we are new creations in Christ, when we are so definitely alive to the old man. The earlier reckoning, concerning our assurance of salvation and security in Christ, is preparation for the later reckoning in regard to identification.

Diligent reliance upon the specific truth of the Word, in the face of all else to the contrary, is our only ground for rest. We cannot cease from self in any other way. We cannot even rest in Christ apart from counting upon the revelation of God's Word. No matter how far we progress in our growth, there will always be a degree of this "labor" involved — turning from the testimony of the temporal, to the eternal witness of Scripture. This is especially necessary because self will never change; it will always be sinful, never possessed of one good thing. We must ever count upon the *exchange* of the cross to separate us from the influence of self, freeing us to rest in the life of our Lord.

Knowing, and resting in, the finished work of our identification causes us to be neither slack, nor self-confident. Rather, knowing what He has done *for* us on the cross, and *with* us in Christ, makes us all the more hungry and eager to know experientially what is already ours positionally. "Being confident of this very thing, that he which hath begun a good work in you will perform it until the day of Jesus Christ" (Phil. 1:6).

There is every scriptural reason about us to be perfectly

confident in the Lord Jesus for our growth to maturity, and not to be discouraged by the length of time it takes or by the unchangeableness of self. We are "called according to his purpose. For whom he did foreknow, he also did predestinate to be conformed to the image of his Son" (Rom. 8:28,29). "Faithful is he that calleth you, who also will do it" (1 Thess. 5:24). "For it is God which worketh in you both to will and to do of his good pleasure" (Phil. 2:13).

His dealings with us for our growth, especially as He makes us a "grain of wheat" to fall into the ground and die, may not be very "restful"; but our rest is in Him, and in the precise statements of His Word. We abide in Christ during the *processing* required for us to be brought to the fulfillment of His purpose; we do not fret and struggle because we are not mature the moment we see His standard for us in the Word.

There is another very important aspect of rest. This has to do with our *witness to others*. When we first begin to receive some of the benefit of reckoning, we are bent upon teaching the truths of identification immediately. We know just the ones who need victory! It is easy to forget how long it took for us to come to the threshold of this realm of reckoning, and how thoroughly we had to be *prepared* before we were at all interested in the so-called "deeper truths." But we soon discover that there are very few believers who are responsive.

It is wise to remain comparatively quiet about the liberating truths for the first year or so following our awakening. After a period of reckoning and deeper study, we will not only know better what to share, but how, when, and with whom. Our teaching should be in the attitude of sharing. "If thou put the brethren in remembrance of these things, thou shalt be a good minister of Jesus Christ, nourished up in the words of faith and of good doctrine, *whereunto thou hast attained*" (1 Tim. 4:6).

Once we begin to reckon, some of us make the mistake of seeking to straighten out our pastor and the church along these lines. But our testimony must first be observed by others, and then heard. Only hungry, prepared hearts can receive. Often, barriers are raised by premature teaching; these may take years to remove, and sometimes they are never overcome. It is best to go slowly — at His pace — and make progress that abides.

Actually, the pulpit is not the ideal medium for sharing the truths of identification. No matter how sound and alive a congregation may be, there are only a few individuals at any one time who are ready to enter into the truths of the cross. The Spirit would have us prayerfully watch for the hungry heart, feeding the few in preference to offending the many. Furthermore, those about us have a right to observe over a period of time whether or not our witness and our walk are valid. "And let us not be weary in well doing: for in due season we shall reap, if we faint not" (Gal. 6:9).

Chapter 14

Results of Reckoning

It should be evident by now that the truths we have been studying are interrelated, and interdependent. Together, they form a single unit of truth — centered in the cross and our risen Lord. Their express purpose is to conform us to the image of God's Son. To consolidate and conclude our study, let us consider a few of the *results of reckoning*.

The Continuity of the Cross

"Reckon ye also yourselves to be dead unto sin" (Rom. 6:11, ASV). Having reckoned upon a finished work, we must be prepared to experience the results of the position taken. Counting ourselves to have died unto sin at Calvary is synonymous with taking up that cross. It is to be expected that the result of this is *daily crucifixion*. In this connection, the principle of distinctions in Chapter 10 is to be remembered: our dead-unto-sin reckoning includes two factors — the old man as crucified, and the new man as having died unto sin.

The old man crucified. Our reckoning the old man as crucified results in the Spirit's leading us daily in the path of the cross. He allows us, chiefly through our own mistakes and willfulness, to become enmeshed in situations and circumstances that hold the self-life on the cross, that crucify it and break its power. There is nothing easy or pleasant about the cross, but we learn to *glory* in it because its crucifying power frees us from the "law of sin and death" (Rom. 8:2).

The new man dead unto sin. As we exercise the reckoning-attitude of having died unto sin, and hence take up our cross daily, the result is that we enjoy increasingly the freedom and the abundance of our new life in the risen Lord. We find that the death which we passed through at Calvary now stands between us and the grip of sin and self. In our *standing*, we count upon the crucifixion of the old Adamic source; in our *state*, we find ourselves "alway delivered unto death for Jesus' sake" (2 Cor. 4:11). This dying daily *both* holds the self-life crucified, and manifests the Christ-life in us. *The continuity of the cross in our lives produces continual freedom from the reign of sin.*

The Continuity of Manifestation

"Reckon ye also yourselves to be . . . alive unto God in Christ Jesus" (Rom. 6:11, ASV). The foremost reason for reckoning ourselves to be in the glorified Lord is that His risen life may be *manifested*. Although our "life is hid with Christ in God," His life is not meant to be hid in us!

The wonderful fact about this reckoning is that out of our being "alway delivered unto death," out of our "being made conformable unto His death," His resurrection life emerges. As long as we are in this unredeemed body, which is vulnerable to temptation and prone to sin, we are going to have to count upon the crucifixion of the cross to deal continually with the Adamic life within. But the very things that crucify provide the daily death from which our new life in Christ is revealed. The more death, the more life! "For we which live are alway delivered unto death for Jesus' sake, that the life also of Jesus might be made manifest in our mortal flesh" (2

79

Cor. 4:11). *The continuity of manifestation has its source in our continual conformity to His death*.

The Continuity of Life Out of Death

"So then death worketh in us, but life in you" (2 Cor. 4:12). This is the cumulative result of our *life-out-of-death reckoning*. What is the essential characteristic of the Lord Jesus that is to be manifested in us? It is the *sacrificial* quality of being poured out for others. We are not struggling believers who barely exist until we finally fall into heaven; we are recipients of resurrection life for ourselves, and sacrificial life unto all! "I am come that they might have life, and that they might have it more abundantly" (John 10:10).

When we reckon ourselves alive unto God in our risen Lord, we are thereby taking our position as seated with Him in the heavenlies. We know that the anchor and source of our life is safely and eternally hid with Christ in God. We are assured that nothing, and no one, can touch us apart from His blessed will (Rom. 8:35-39). Our attitude is that of *looking down* upon all that He takes us through — we are not under His circumstances, but above them all in our victorious Lord. Standing in our position, we learn in whatever state we are in, "therewith to be content"; we learn how to be abased, and we learn how to abound (Phil. 4:11,12).

We enter each day (even Monday), and each situation, from that blessed vantage point. Resting in our risen Lord gives us rest in our pilgrim path. We abide in Him, accepting everything from His nail-pierced hands. *"In* everything give thanks: for this is the will of God in Christ Jesus concerning you" (1 Thess. 5:18).

Always to be remembered is the fact that the One in whom we live in glory is forever viewed as "a Lamb as it had been slain" (Rev. 5:6). While we abide in and reckon upon our life in the Lamb of God, and are taken through the Spirit's processing, His sacrificial lamblike qualities will be manifested in and through us. Death works in us, but life in others.

Another blessed result of being alway delivered unto death is *a growing knowledge, by experience, of our crucified, risen Lord*. As the Holy Spirit delivers us day by day unto the path of the cross, we suffer infirmities, reproaches, necessities, persecutions, and distresses "for Jesus' sake." "That I may know him" is closely related to "the fellowship of his sufferings" (Phil. 3:10). Our confidence in the Lord Jesus develops as we realize that His grace is sufficient for all these things, and that His strength is made perfect in our weakness (2 Cor. 12:9,10). We are compelled to prove His faithfulness at every point of need.

Although we are living in our risen Lord, we are camping in this body of humiliation, and serving in this world of death. Therefore, our Father keeps us in the place of need and helplessness in ourselves. "We have this treasure in earthen vessels, that the excellency of the power may be of God, and not of us" (2 Cor. 4:7). As we are kept dependent, we grow in His submissive, yielded life. "I come to do thy will, O God" (Heb. 10:9). Abiding in the Lord Jesus, it is effortless and natural to yield. The only struggle in the matter of yielding erupts from the self-life; that source never was, never will be, nor ever can be, in subjection to the Father (Rom. 8:7).

Paul's urgent plea for the believer's yielding and consecration is based upon reckoning. "I beseech you therefore, brethren, by the mercies of God, that ye present your bodies

81

a living sacrifice" (Rom. 12:1). To present our bodies is to yield our faculties, our new life in Christ. "Yield yourselves unto God, as those that are alive from the dead [new creation], and your members as instruments of righteousness unto God" (Rom. 6:13). Life-out-of-death reckoning results in our becoming a "living sacrifice." Such a one is always delivered unto death — but, out of that daily death, new life is constantly manifested.

Our reckoning maintains us in *the life-out-of-death principle*. This taking up our cross renders us a "grain of wheat," and results in our losing our old life. The Holy Spirit "buries" us here in this situation and there in that location, so that we might not abide alone but that there may be a rich harvest of golden grain "for Jesus' sake." It is comforting to realize that the same process of the cross that holds the old man crucified, causes the new man to be manifest. The burial of the "grain of wheat" makes the old life powerless, and the new life fruitful (John 12:24,25, ASV).

Some of the "graves" out of which His sacrificial life arises are the ministry, the mission field, the home, the school, the hospital, and the place of employment. Are these not the very places in which His resurrection life must be manifested, where His poured-out life needs to be shared and received? It is as we reckon upon our heavenly position that we are able to rest in any "grave" He has prepared for us, rejoicing in His victory that emerges from our daily deliverance unto death. We abide in the Lord Jesus, that He may bring us through all the processing required for fruitful life and service, "not somehow, but triumphantly."

Hereby we learn that "all things are for your sakes, that the abundant grace might through the thanksgiving of many redound to the glory of God. For which cause we faint not; but though our outward man perish, yet the inward man [new man] is renewed day by day" (2 Cor. 4:15,16). "And we know that all things work together for good to them that love God, to them who are the called according to his purpose. For whom he did foreknow, he also did predestinate to be conformed to the image of his Son" (Rom. 8:28,29).

Take heart, reckoning pilgrim! The *continuity of life out of death leads to the Crown*. "It is a faithful saying: For if we be dead with him, we shall also live with him: If we suffer, we shall also reign with him" (2 Tim. 2:11,12). "When Christ, who is our life, shall appear, then shall ye also appear with him in *glory*" (Col. 3:4). Maranatha!

(Appendix)
Foundation of
Reckoning

Reckoning upon our life-union with the Lord Jesus Christ establishes us in the full *assurance* of salvation. On this foundation we are able to reckon upon our *eternal, unconditional security* in Him. Until we are grounded in the truths of substitution and union, we are not prepared for the more demanding reckoning of our *identification* with Him in His death and resurrection — and on to ascension.

The believer who does not realize that he is eternally secure in Christ — a birth truth for babes — is certainly not going to be able to trust Him for emancipation from sin and maturity of growth. Those who begin weakly, and are not instructed concerning their *position* in the Lord Jesus, are apt to remain weaklings. They move mainly up, down, and backward, with rarely any forward spiritual progress and abiding growth. For the most part, they subsist on experiences and so-called blessings; they seem to go from one crisis to another, never really settling down to reckon upon Christ risen as the source of their life here and now.

It has been felt necessary to include the following selected material on Eternal Security (author unknown). These truths may be of help to any believers who are attempting to enter upon the reckoning of identification before they are settled in that of *justification*.

"If you recognize in the Word of Truth

> that the Lord Jesus Christ is the Saviour because He is God the Son who became the Son of Man, and as such bore in His body the sins of the world;

"And if you rest in Him

> in self-surrender for fellowship, relying with confidence on Him alone for deliverance from the guilt and penalty of your sins and from the power of indwelling sin:

"Then there are *twelve proofs* that you can never be lost:

1. Because in the eternal, sure *purpose of God*, you are a 'vessel of mercy' and will finally be 'conformed to the image of His Son.' 'That He might make known the riches of His glory on the vessels of mercy, which He had afore prepared unto glory.' 'For whom He did foreknow, He also did predestinate to be conformed to the image of His Son' (Rom. 9:23; 8:29).

2. Because *God's infinite power* is no longer hindered by your sins, but can wholly keep you safe, for the Blood of Christ still removes your guilt. 'He is the propitiation for our sins' (1 John 2:2).

3. Because *God's love* for you, supremely expressed at Calvary, can now be manifested 'much more' and so accomplish His every desire for you. 'God commendeth His love toward us, in that, while we were yet sinners, Christ died for us. Much more then, being justified by His Blood, we shall be saved from wrath

85

through Him. For if, when we were enemies, we were reconciled to God by the death of His Son, much more being reconciled, we shall be saved by His life' (Rom. 5:8-10).

4. Because of His delight in the Son, God can never reject the *prayer of the Son* asking Him to keep 'them which Thou hast given Me.' 'I pray for them . . . for they are Thine.' 'Holy Father, keep through Thine own Name those whom Thou hast given Me' (John 17:9,11).

5. Because the *death of the Son*, having a value equivalent to the punishment demanded for all your sins, has paid also for sins you now commit. 'There is therefore now no condemnation to them which are in Christ Jesus.' 'Who is he that condemneth? It is Christ that died, yea rather, that is risen again, who is even at the right hand of God, who also maketh intercession for us' (Rom. 8:1,34).

6. Because by the *resurrection of Christ* God has broken your connection with Adam and joined you to Christ for acceptance and life. 'You, being dead in your sins . . . hath He quickened [enlifed] together with Him, having forgiven you all trespasses.' 'Yield yourselves unto God, as those that are alive from the dead' (Col. 2:13; Rom. 6:13).

7. Because, although your sin could hurl you into hell, Christ as your *Advocate* defends you. 'Christ is . . . entered . . . into heaven itself, now to appear in the presence of God for us.' 'Now once in the end of the world hath He appeared to put away sin by the sacrifice of Himself' (Heb. 9:24,26).

8. Because Christ 'ever liveth *to make intercession*' for you, Satan has no power to unsave you. 'He is able also to save them to the uttermost that come unto God by Him, seeing He ever liveth to make intercession for them' (Heb. 7:25).

9. Because the Holy Spirit has taken over your body as *His personal, permanent home*. 'I will pray the Father, and He shall give you another Comforter, that He may abide with you forever' (John 14:16).

10. Because the Holy Spirit has planted in you *the very life of God*, making God your real Father. 'Which were born, not of blood, nor of the will of the flesh, nor of the will of man, but of God' (John 1:13).

11. Because the Holy Spirit has now united you with Christ and you are *a very part of Himself*. 'For by one Spirit are we all baptized into one Body' (1 Cor. 12:13).

12. Because the Holy Spirit in you is the *seal* that your salvation is a finished transaction. 'Grieve not the Holy Spirit of God, whereby ye are sealed unto the day of redemption' (Eph. 4:30).

"Though your present sins cannot unsave you, remember there are *other penalties* you bring upon yourself, the least of which is chastisement at your Father's hand." "Do not faint when He corrects you; for those whom the Lord loves He disciplines" (Heb. 12:6, Wey.).

Further, "to accept and teach that a Blood-bought child of God can fall from grace is to assault the very *nature*, *character*, and *sovereign purpose* of God, as well as His *justice* and His *love*.

"Such teaching is an assault on the *nature* of God in that believers are declared to be 'partakers of the divine nature' (2 Pet. 1:4); 'born, not of blood, nor of the will of the flesh, nor of the will of man, but of God' (John 1:13); and indwelt by the Holy Spirit of God (John 14:16,17).

"It is an assault on the *character* of God — His faithfulness and truthfulness, in that the life He imparts He gives His pledge to maintain. His promise is, 'I give unto them eternal life; and they shall never perish, neither shall any man pluck them out of My hand' (John 10:28): 'and shall not come into condemnation; but *is* passed from death unto life' (John 5:24).

"Also, the doctrine of 'falling from grace' is an assault on the *sovereign purpose* of God as set forth in Romans 8:28-30, where the believer is seen in the purpose of God in the eternity of the past, in His foreknowledge and predestination, and in the eternity of the future sharing the very glory of Christ (John 17:22-26).

"Then, it is an assault on the *justice* of God, in that God declares concerning the believer, 'Your life is hid with Christ in God' (Col. 3:3), and that there is now 'no condemnation to them which are in Christ Jesus,' and no separation 'from the love of God, which is in Christ Jesus our Lord' (Rom. 8:1, 37-39). Thus, we can thank our Heavenly Father for His justice, for it is this which preserves the child of God from a second charge:

'Payment, God cannot twice demand,
First at my bleeding Surety's hand,
And then again at mine.'

"Lastly, it is an assault on the *love* of God, in that God declares His love 'an everlasting love' from which nothing 'shall be able to separate,' for He is 'able to keep you from falling, and to present you faultless before the presence of His glory with exceeding joy' (Jer. 31:3; Rom. 8:39; Jude 24)."